JESUS REVEALED
LEADER GUIDE

JESUS REVEALED

The I Am Statements in the Gospel of John

Jesus Revealed

978-1-7910-2460-4

978-1-7910-2461-1 eBook

Jesus Revealed: Leader Guide

978-1-7910-2462-8

978-1-7910-2463-5 eBook

Jesus Revealed: DVD

978-1-7910-2464-2

ALSO BY MATT RAWLE

The Heart That Grew Three Sizes

The Redemption of Scrooge

The Grace of Les Miserables

The Gift of the Nutcracker

Hollywood Jesus

The Faith of a Mockingbird

The Salvation of Doctor Who

FOR MORE INFORMATION, VISIT MATTRAWLE.COM.

MATT RAWLE

JESUS REVEALED

THE I AM STATEMENTS
IN THE GOSPEL OF JOHN

LEADER GUIDE

ABINGDON PRESS | NASHVILLE

Jesus Revealed

The I Am Statements in the Gospel of John

Leader Guide

Copyright © 2022 Abingdon Press
All rights reserved.

978-1-7910-2462-8

MANUFACTURED IN THE UNITED STATES OF AMERICA

CONTENTS

TO THE LEADER

In *Jesus Revealed: The I Am Statements in the Gospel of John*, author Matt Rawle explores the seven I Am statements found in John's Gospel, in which Jesus uses rich metaphors to paint a clear picture of who he is. By exploring these I Am statements, we come to see multiple layers of Jesus's identity and the way we are called to respond in faith.

John's Gospel is a work of art, and it is best read with an appreciation for its drama, use of symbolism and imagery, and a story that builds to the resurrection of Jesus. In the book, you will find that each chapter is structured as follows:

- The Scene, which explores the immediate context in which Jesus utters the I Am statement.
- The Act, which explores the I Am statement within the context of the Gospel of John and the other Gospels.
- The Play, which explores the I Am statement in light of all of Scripture.

- Your Role, which explores how we fit into the story and how God calls us to participate in it.

This Leader Guide follows the same structure, providing an in-depth look at each I Am statement. It is designed to help leaders of adult Christian small groups to discuss and learn from *Jesus Revealed* and apply its lessons to their lives. There are six sessions, corresponding to the six chapters of the book:

1. I Am the Light of the World (John 8:12)
2. I Am the Bread of Life (John 6:35)
3. I Am the Good Shepherd (also includes I Am the Gate of the Sheep; John 10:7 and 10:11)
4. I Am the Vine (John 15:5)
5. I Am the Way, the Truth, and the Life (John 14:6)
6. I Am the Resurrection and the Life (John 11:25)

HOW TO FACILITATE THIS STUDY

This study makes use of the following components:

- *Jesus Revealed: The I Am Statements in the Gospel of John,* by Matt Rawle.
- This *Leader Guide*.
- *Jesus Revealed DVD*, or access to the streaming video sessions via Amplify Media (www.amplifymedia.com). The video features Matt Rawle teaching the content of each chapter, as well as short artistic videos by Louisiana-based artist Sarah Duet and inspired by the I Am statements.
- **The Bible.** A variety of translations are both allowable and desirable in your small group. Multiple translations allow you to compare wording and open the possibility for new insights into the text. Some great translations include the Common English Bible (CEB), New Revised Standard Version (NRSV), and New International Version (NIV).

Each session should take approximately 45–60 minutes to complete and consists of the following segments:

- **Session Goals:** Describes the objectives of this week's lesson.
- **Biblical Foundation:** Contains the key Scripture texts for this week's lesson.
- **Preparation:** Contains the preparation steps to complete in advance of each session.
- **Opening the Session:** Gather the group together, introduce the main ideas for this lesson with a brief discussion or activity, then open with prayer.
- **Watch the Video:** Watch the video session and discuss, using the questions provided.
- **Scripture and Book Study:** Discuss the Scripture passage and the relevant chapter of *Jesus Revealed* using the discussion questions that are provided in each section.
- **Closing the Session: Your Role**: Wrap up the session with a closing discussion and end with prayer.

HELPFUL HINTS

PREPARING FOR EACH SESSION

- Carefully read the corresponding chapter of *Jesus Revealed*.
- Prayerfully read the session's Biblical Foundation, noting questions and issues you need or want to study further. Consult trusted biblical references for more information.
- Gather Bibles for participants (or slides of the session's Biblical Foundation for screen-sharing purposes , or both), as well as paper or notebooks for people to write their responses when invited.
- Review the discussion questions for the session and select the ones you want to spend the most time with in your

group. Be prepared, however, to adjust the session as
group members interact and as questions arise. Prepare
carefully but allow space for the Holy Spirit to move in
and through the group members and through you as
facilitator.

- Prepare the space where the group will meet so that the
space will enhance the learning process. Ideally, group
members should be seated around a table or in a circle so
that all can see one another.

SHAPING THE LEARNING ENVIRONMENT

- Create a climate of openness, encouraging group members
to participate as they feel comfortable.
- Remember that some people will jump right in with
answers and comments, while others need time to process
what is being discussed.
- If you notice that some group members seem never to
be able to enter the conversation, ask them if they have
thoughts to share. Give everyone a chance to talk but
keep the conversation moving. Moderate to prevent a few
individuals from doing all the talking.
- Communicate the importance of group discussions and
group exercises.
- If no one answers at first during discussions, do not
be afraid of silence. Count silently to ten, then say
something such as, "Would anyone like to go first?" If
no one responds, venture an answer yourself and ask for
comments.
- Model openness as you share with the group. Group
members will follow your example. If you limit your
sharing to a surface level, others will follow suit.
- Encourage multiple answers or responses before moving on
to the next question.

- Ask: "Why?" or "Why do you believe that?" or "Can you say more about that?" to help continue a discussion and give it greater depth.
- Affirm others' responses with comments such as "Great" or "Thanks" or "Good insight"—especially if it's the first time someone has spoken during the group session.
- Monitor your own contributions. If you are doing most of the talking, back off so that you do not train the group to listen rather than speak up.
- Remember that you do not have to have all the answers. Your job is to keep the discussion going and encourage participation.

MANAGING THE SESSION

- Honor the time schedule. If a session is running longer than expected, get consensus from the group before continuing beyond the agreed-upon ending time.
- Involve group members in various aspects of the group session, such as saying prayers or reading the Scripture.
- As always in discussions that may involve personal sharing, confidentiality is essential. Group members should never pass along stories that have been shared in the group. Remind the group members at each session: confidentiality is crucial to the success of this study.

ADAPTING FOR VIRTUAL SMALL GROUP SESSIONS

Meeting online is a great option for a number of situations. During a time of a public-health hazard, such as the COVID-19 pandemic, online meetings are a welcome opportunity for people to converse while seeing one another's faces. Online meetings can also expand the "neighborhood" of possible group members, because people can log in from just about anywhere in the world. This also gives those who do not have access to transportation or who prefer not to travel at certain times of day the chance to participate.

The guidelines below will help you lead an effective and enriching group study using an online video conferencing platform such as Zoom, Webex, Google Meet, Microsoft Teams, or another virtual meeting platform of your choice.

BASIC FEATURES FOR VIRTUAL MEETINGS

There are many choices for videoconferencing platforms. You may have personal experience and comfort using a particular service, or your church may have a subscription that will influence your choice. Whichever option you choose, it is recommended that you use a platform that supports the following features:

- **Synchronous video and audio:** Your participants can see and speak to one another live, in real time. Participants have the ability to turn their video off and on, and to mute and unmute their audio.
- **Chat:** Your participants can send text messages to the whole group or individuals from within the virtual meeting. Participants can put active hyperlinks (that is, "clickable" internet addresses) into the chat for other participants' convenience.
- **Screen-Sharing:** Participants can share the contents of their screen with other participants (the meeting host's permission may be required).
- **Video Sharing:** Participants (or the host) can share videos and computer audio via screen share, so that all participants can view the videos each week.
- **Breakout Rooms:** Meeting hosts can automatically or manually send participants into virtual smaller groups and can determine whether the rooms end automatically

after a set period of time. Hosts can communicate with all breakout rooms. *This feature is useful if your group is large, or if you wish to break into smaller teams of two or three for certain activities. If you have a smaller group, this feature may not be necessary.*

Check with your pastor or director of discipleship to see if your church has a preferred platform or an account with one or more of these platforms that you might use. In most instances, only the host will need to be signed in to the account; others can participate without being registered.

Zoom, Webex, Google Meet, and Microsoft Teams all offer free versions of their platform, which you can use if your church doesn't have an account. However, there may be some restrictions (for instance, Zoom's free version limits meetings to 45 minutes). Check each platform's website to be sure you are aware of any such restrictions before you sign up.

Once you have selected a platform, familiarize yourself with all of its features and controls so that you can facilitate virtual meetings comfortably. The platform's website will have lists of features and helpful tutorials, often third-party sites will have useful information or instructions as well.

There are additional features on many platforms that help play your video more effectively. In Zoom, for example, as you click the "share screen" option and see the screen showing your different windows, check at the bottom of that window to choose "optimize for video clips" and "share audio." These ensure that your group hears the audio and that, when using a clip, the video resolution is compressed to fit the bandwidth that you have.

In addition to videoconferencing software, it is also advisable to have access to slide-creation software such as Microsoft PowerPoint or Google Slides. These can be used to prepare easy slides for screen-sharing to display discussion questions, quotes from the study book, or Scripture passages. If you don't have easy access to these, you can create a document and share it—but make sure the print size is easy to read.

VIDEO SHARING

For a video-based study, it's important to be able to screen-share your videos so that all participants can view them in your study session. The good news is, whether you have the videos on DVD or streaming files, it is possible to play them in your session.

All the videoconferencing platforms mentioned above support screen-sharing videos. Some have specific requirements for assuring that sound will play clearly in addition to the videos. Follow your videoconferencing platform instructions carefully, and test the video sharing in advance to be sure it works.

If you wish to screen-share a DVD video, you may need to use a different media player. Some media players will not allow you to share your screen when you play copyright-protected DVDs. VLC is a free media player that is safe and easy to use. To try this software, download at videolan.org/VLC.

What about copyright? DVDs like those you use for group study are meant to be used in a group setting in "real time." That is, whether you meet in person, online, or in a hybrid setting, Abingdon Press encourages use of your DVD or streaming video.

What is allowed: Streaming an Abingdon DVD over Zoom, Teams, or similar platform during a small group session.

What is not allowed: Posting video of a published DVD study to social media or YouTube for later viewing.

If you have any questions about permissions and copyright, email permissions@abingdonpress.com.

Amplify Media. The streaming subscription platform Amplify Media makes it easy to share streaming videos for groups. When your church has an Amplify subscription, your group members can sign on and have access to the video sessions. With access, they may watch the video on their own ahead of your group meeting, watch the streaming video during your group meeting, or view it again after the meeting. Thousands of videos are on AmplifyMedia.com making it easy to watch anytime, anywhere, and on any device from phones and tablets to Smart TVs and desktops.

Visit AmplifyMedia.com to learn more or call 1-800-672-1789, option 4, to hear about the current offers.

COMMUNICATING WITH YOUR GROUP

Clear communication with your small group before and throughout your study is crucial no matter how you meet, but it is doubly important if you are gathering virtually.

Advertising the Study. Be sure to advertise your virtual study either on your church's website or in its newsletter, or both, as well as any social media that your church uses. Request pastors or other worship leaders announce it in worship services.

Registration. Encourage people to register for the online study so that you can know all participants and have a way to contact them. Ideally, you will collect an email address for each participant so that you can send them communications and links to your virtual meeting sessions. An event-planning tool such as SignUpGenius makes this easy and gives you a database of participants and their email addresses.

Welcome Email. Before your first session, several days in advance, send an email to everyone who has registered for the study, welcoming them to the group, reminding them of the date and time of your first meeting, and including a link to join the virtual meeting. It's also a good idea to include one or two discussion questions to "prime the pump" for reflection and conversation when you gather.

If you have members without internet service, or if they are uncomfortable using a computer and videoconferencing software, let them know they may telephone into the meeting. Provide them the number and let them know that there is usually a unique phone number for each meeting.

Weekly Emails. Send a new email two or three days before each week's session, again including the link to join your virtual meeting and one or two discussion questions to set the stage for discussion. Feel free to use any of the questions in the Leader Guide for this purpose. If you find a particular quote from the book that is especially meaningful, include this as well.

Facebook. Consider creating a private Facebook group for your small group, where you can hold discussion and invite reflection between your weekly meetings. Each week, post one or two quotes from the study book along with a short question for reflection and invite people to respond in the comments. These questions can come straight from the Leader Guide, and you can revisit the Facebook conversation during your virtual meeting.

You might also consider posting these quotes and questions on your church's main Facebook page, inviting people in your congregation beyond your small group to join the conversation. This can be a great way to involve others in your study, or to let people know about it and invite them to join your next virtual meeting.

DURING YOUR VIRTUAL SESSIONS

During your virtual sessions, follow these tips to be sure you are prepared and that everything runs as smoothly as possible.

GETTING READY

- Familiarize yourself with the controls and features of your videoconferencing platform, using instructions or tutorials available via the platform's website or third-party sites.
- Be sure you are leading the session from a well-lit place in front of a background free from excessive distractions.
- As leader, log in to the virtual meeting early. You want to be a good host who is present to welcome participants by name as they arrive. This also gives you time to check how

you appear on camera, so that you can make any last-minute adjustments to your lighting and background if needed.

CREATING COMMUNITY ONLINE

- During each session, pay attention to who is speaking and who is not. Because of video and audio lags as well as internet connections of varying quality, some participants may inadvertently speak over one another without realizing they are doing so. As needed, directly prompt specific people to speak if they wish (for example, "Alan, it looked like you were about to say something when Sarah was speaking").

- If your group is especially large, you may want to agree with members on a procedure for being recognized to speak (for example, participants might "raise hands" digitally or type "call on me" in the chat feature).

- Instruct participants to keep their microphones muted during the meeting, so extraneous noise from their location does not interrupt the meeting. This includes chewing or yawning sounds, which can be embarrassing! When it is time for discussion, participants can unmute themselves.

- Remember some participants may wish to simply observe and listen—do not pressure anyone to speak who does not wish to.

- Always get your group's permission before recording your online sessions. While those who are unable to attend the meeting may appreciate the chance to view it later, respect the privacy of your participants.

- Communicate with your group in between sessions with weekly emails and Facebook posts to spark ongoing discussion.

In challenging times, modern technology has powerful potential to bring God's people together in new and nourishing ways. May such be your experience during this virtual study.

HELP, SUPPORT, AND TUTORIALS

The creators of the most popular virtual meeting platforms have excellent, free resources available online to help you get started using their platform, which teach you everything from how to join a meeting as a participant to how to use the more advanced features like video sharing and breakout rooms. Most of them offer clear written instructions as well as video tutorials and also provide a way to contact the company in case you need additional assistance.

Below are links for five platforms: Zoom, Microsoft Teams, Webex, Google Meet, and GoTo Meeting. If you are using a different platform, go to their website and look for the "Help" or "Resources" page.

- **Zoom Help Center**
  https://support.zoom.us/hc/en-us
  Contains a comprehensive collection of resources to help
  you use the Zoom platform, including quick start guides,
  video tutorials, articles, and specific sets of instructions on
  various topics or issues you may run into.
- **Microsoft Teams Help & Learning**
  https://support.microsoft.com/en-us/teams
  A collection of articles, videos, and instructions on how to
  use the Microsoft Teams platform. Teams offers a number
  of features. You are most likely to find the help you need
  for group meetings by navigating to the "Meetings" page,
  or by clicking "Microsoft Teams training" under "Explore
  Microsoft Teams."

- **Webex Help Center**
  https://help.webex.com/en-us/
  Contains articles, videos, and other resources to help you use the Webex platform, with everything from joining the meeting to screen-sharing and using a virtual whiteboard.
- **Google Meet Help**
  https://support.google.com/meet/
  Contains a list of support topics to help you use the Google Meet platform in an easy-to-read expandable list that makes it easy to find just what you need.
- **GoTo Meeting Support**
  https://support.goto.com/meeting
  Here you'll find links with instructions on various topics to help you use the GoTo Meeting platform.

GENERAL HOW-TO

In addition to these official support pages, there are numerous independent sites online with great, clear instructions on using multiple platforms. Here is one excellent resource:

- **Nerds Chalk**
  https://nerdschalk.com/
  This site is easily searchable and contains numerous articles and how-go guides, with clear titles to help you find exactly what you need. Simply search for either your chosen platform or what you are trying to accomplish such as "Breakout rooms" or "Zoom screen share," and navigate to the most relevant link.

1

I AM THE LIGHT
OF THE WORLD

PLANNING THE SESSION

SESSION GOALS

Through this session's discussion and activities, participants will be encouraged to:

- appreciate the Gospel of John as a rich work of art;
- recognize Jesus as the fully divine, eternal light of the world;
- explore the symbolism of light and darkness throughout John's Gospel and all of Scripture; and
- understand the things that can blind us spiritually and how we can begin to see Christ clearly.

BIBLICAL FOUNDATION

- John 1:1-5
- John 8:12
- John 9:1-41

PREPARATION

- Read the introduction and chapter 1, "I Am the Light of the World" in *Jesus Revealed*, by Matt Rawle, making note of anything that stands out to you.
- Read through this Leader Guide session to familiarize yourself with it and to decide which questions you will cover.
- Read and reflect on the Biblical Foundation passages listed above.
- Preview the Session 1 video and make arrangements to play, using a DVD player or computer, during your session.
- Set up a markerboard or large sheet of paper for recording group members' ideas.
- Have a Bible, paper for taking notes, and a pen or pencil available for every participant.
- Provide nametags and markers.
- Provide extra copies of *Jesus Revealed*.

OPENING THE SESSION

Greet and welcome participants as they arrive. Invite them to make a nametag and pick up either a Bible or a copy of *Jesus Revealed*, or both, if they did not bring their own.

Introduce yourself and share why you are excited to lead this study of *Jesus Revealed* and the I Am statements in the Gospel of John. Invite all group members to introduce themselves and share what they hope to learn in this study.

Begin your discussion with the following questions:

- Think about images or metaphors you have encountered about Jesus. Which ones do you find most powerful? Why? (*Examples may include Jesus welcoming children, Jesus as a healer, Jesus as a teacher, Jesus as a shepherd, Jesus on the cross, and so on.*)
- How does each image communicate something different about who Jesus is?

Say: In this study we will discuss seven statements in the Gospel of John where Jesus describes himself symbolically:

- "I am the light of the world" (8:12)
- "I am the bread of life" (6:35)
- "I am the gate of the sheep" (10:7)
- "I am the good shepherd" (10:11)
- "I am the vine; you are the branches" (15:5)
- "I am the way, the truth, and the life" (14:6)
- "I am the resurrection and the life" (11:25)

As we will see over the next six weeks, these images work together to give us a multilayered view of who Jesus is and what his life, death, and resurrection mean for us and for the world. In today's session we will explore "I am the light of the world" (John 8:12).

OPENING PRAYER

Pray the following prayer or one of your own:

Lord Jesus, we believe that you are the light of the world. Open our eyes that we may see you clearly, and so that we may see the world clearly because of who you are. Guide our study and our conversation today and throughout the next six weeks. Reveal yourself to us so that we may know you and be known by you; in your name we pray. Amen.

WATCH THE VIDEO

Play the video for session 1 using your DVD player or stream with Amplify Media. Discuss the following questions:

- What stood out to you as you watched the video?
- Matt Rawle describes the blindness of the Pharisees after Jesus heals the man born blind. We all have a tendency toward spiritual blindness. What might you be blind to?
- Matt Rawle invites us to see the Gospel of John as a work of art. How does it change your perspective to see John in this way? Do any other books or passages of Scripture seem artistic to you?
- What thoughts, feelings, or images came to you as you watched the ending clip of artist Sarah Duet painting a picture inspired by "I am light"?

Invite the group to keep both the video and the book in mind throughout the discussion below.

SCRIPTURE AND BOOK STUDY

THE LIGHT OF THE WORLD

Invite a volunteer to read John 8:12-20. Discuss:

- What do you think Jesus means by describing himself as "the light of the world"?
- How do the Pharisees react to Jesus's statement? What does this say about what is important to them?

Read the following quote aloud and discuss:

Ultimately, light is passive. Light is meant to illuminate everything but itself. Jesus says, "I am the light of the world. Whoever follows me will never walk in darkness but will have the light of life" (John 8:12). The light goes ahead of us, revealing where to walk. If we stare directly at the light, we actually stumble. The same rocks and divots will catch our feet, just as if our eyes are closed or if there wasn't any light at all. Light is meant to illuminate our surroundings so that we can clearly see the way we are meant to go. (p. 4)

- How did the Pharisees' focus on Jesus prevent them from seeing clearly?
- What questions or attitudes about Jesus today might prevent us from seeing clearly?

THE SCENE: BLIND FROM BIRTH

Divide your group into pairs. Have each pair work together to read John 9:1-41 and identify where they see tension between light and dark, or sight and blindness, in this chapter. Allow 5–10 minutes for the pairs to work, then invite each pair to report what they found. Record the various responses on a markerboard or large sheet of paper.

Take a moment to review the responses, then discuss:

- How did the blind man's understanding of Jesus grow over the course of this chapter?
- Do the Pharisees and others in the story increase their understanding of Jesus and the miracle that has occurred, or does their understanding decrease? Why?
- Sometimes, thinking we have all the answers can prevent us from seeing clearly. In what ways might your spiritual vision and understanding be limited?
- What can you do to open yourself to the light of the world and come to see Jesus, and everything else, more clearly?

THE ACT: LIGHT AND LIFE

Invite a volunteer to read aloud John 1:1-14. Discuss:

- What is the relationship between the Word, life, and light in these verses?

- If the Word refers to Jesus, what picture of Jesus does this passage paint? What is the significance of beginning John's Gospel in this way?

Invite the group to consult the section of *Jesus Revealed* under the heading "The Act: Light and Life" (pp. 11–15).

- How does the theme of light and darkness carry through the Gospel of John?
- Which characters see the light most clearly by the end? Which ones seem to remain in darkness, or lack understanding of who Jesus is? Why?
- How do the stories Rawle discusses in this section deepen your understanding of Jesus's statement, "I am the light of the world"?
- Which characters in these stories—Nicodemus, the Samaritan woman, or the disciples—do you most identify with? Why?

THE PLAY: LIGHT FROM THE BEGINNING

Light is an important symbol throughout Scripture. Lead your group in a brainstorming session. See how many examples of light can you recall from the Bible in five minutes.

Set a timer for five minutes and invite the group to share as many instances as possible where light is mentioned in the Bible. Examples can be mundane or symbolic. Write the responses down on a markerboard or large sheet of paper. When time is up, discuss the following:

- What do these examples of light in the Bible say about our relationship with God?
- Which of them point to Jesus as the light of the world? Which do not (or which are a stretch)?
- Matt Rawle notes that "God's grand drama begins and ends with light. If we look at the entirety of the story, we

recognize God's word as narrative about light. If the Bible were a play or a movie, you might describe it as a play about light itself" (p. 20). Do you agree with this idea? Why or why not? What insights do we gain if we understand the Bible in this way? What might we miss?

CLOSING THE SESSION: YOUR ROLE

Read the following quote aloud:

All things were created through God's Word in much the same way that light is the boundary of the universe. Nothing exists outside of its reach. Light also doesn't age. It's timeless. Jesus saying "I am the light of the world" is also another way of saying "I am the Alpha and the Omega, the beginning and end." Christ is the timeless wisdom of God through which all things find being and meaning. (pp. 19–20)

- How can you, as a follower of Christ, find your being and meaning in him more fully?
- The symbol of light teaches us that Jesus is "up there" and "out there"—cosmic and eternal. What hope or comfort do you find in this image? How does it challenge you or give you pause?
- How do you think the other I Am statements we will study will complement this one?

CLOSING PRAYER

End with the following prayer or one of your own:

Eternal God, light of the world. Thank you for being with us today and for lighting our path always. Attune our eyes to see you clearly, and to see the world clearly by the light you provide. We believe and trust that you are the light of the world, and that in you there is life; in Jesus's name we pray. Amen.

I AM THE BREAD OF LIFE

PLANNING THE SESSION

SESSION GOALS

Through this session's discussion and activities, participants will be encouraged to:

- understand how the symbol of bread points to Jesus's humanity;
- eecognize how bread and light round out a picture of Jesus as both fully human and fully divine; and
- appreciate the celebration of Communion as a way to bear witness to Jesus's humanity.

BIBLICAL FOUNDATION

- Exodus 16:1-21
- John 6:1-59

PREPARATION

- Read chapter 2, "I Am the Bread of Life," in *Jesus Revealed*, by Matt Rawle, making note of anything that stands out to you.
- Read through this Leader Guide session to familiarize yourself with it and to decide which questions you will cover.
- Read and reflect on the Biblical Foundation passages listed above.
- Preview the session 2 video and make arrangements to play it, using a DVD player or computer, during your session.
- Set up a markerboard or large sheet of paper for recording group members' ideas.
- Have a Bible, paper for taking notes, and a pen or pencil available for every participant.

OPENING THE SESSION

Greet and welcome participants as they arrive. Invite them to make a nametag and pick up either a Bible or a copy of *Jesus Revealed*, or both, if they did not bring their own.

Give any new members an opportunity to introduce themselves. *Briefly* recap last week's lesson and mention that today's session is on the I Am statement "I am the bread of life."

Begin your discussion with the following questions:

- What is your favorite kind of bread? What makes it special to you?
- How is food in general a part of your faith? In what ways do we incorporate food into our worship, fellowship, service, prayers, or other aspects of public or private faith?

Say: In today's session as we discuss Jesus's statement, "I am the bread of life," we will explore the ways Jesus uses food to tell us about who he is.

OPENING PRAYER

Begin with the following prayer or one of your own:

Lord Jesus, we believe that you are the bread of life. We hunger for many things, from physical food to spiritual nourishment. We know and trust that you provide all these things to us. Today as we ponder your words, "I am the bread of life," help us to recognize that you are the source of it all; in your holy name we pray. Amen.

WATCH THE VIDEO

Play the video for session 2 using your DVD player or stream with Amplify Media. Discuss the following questions:

- What stood out to you as you watched the video?
- What is the difference between a mindset of scarcity and one of abundance? When are you most tempted to approach life with a mindset of scarcity?
- Matt Rawle says that the church has a certain amount of discomfort with the idea that Jesus was fully human. Do you agree? Why does Jesus's humanity make us a little uncomfortable?
- What thoughts, feelings, or images came to you as you listened to Matt Rawle's poem or the video clip of artist Sarah Duet painting a picture inspired by "I am the bread of life"?

Invite the group to keep both the video and the book in mind throughout the discussion below.

SCRIPTURE AND BOOK STUDY

THE SCENE: FEEDING OF THE FIVR THOUSAND

Invite a volunteer to read John 6:1-15. Discuss the following questions:

- Why was the crowd following Jesus? What did they hope to gain from him?
- Compare the responses of Philip and Andrew when Jesus asked about providing food for the gathered crowd. What do these two responses say about the disciples' mindset?
- On pages 29–30, Matt Rawle contrasts a mindset of scarcity with one of abundance. What is the difference between the two? Why is a scarcity mindset so limiting?
- What would be different if you approached life with a posture of abundance?
- How did the crowd respond to Jesus's miraculous feeding of the five thousand? What does this indicate about their perception of Jesus?

Invite a volunteer to read John 6:26-42. Discuss:

- Why does the crowd ask Jesus about manna in the wilderness?
- In what ways does Jesus go beyond what Moses offered the people? What does Jesus offer that Moses did not?
- How does the crowd respond in verses 41-42, after Jesus proclaims that he is "the bread of life"?

Read the following quote aloud:

Instead of celebrating or turning to worship, the crowd complains saying that Jesus is just Joseph's son (John 6:42). Honestly, I can understand some of their frustration. When we understand Jesus to be the light of the world, this divine picture of timelessness and wonder, we might forget that Jesus was also fully human. Jesus had a mother, and an earthly father who raised him. He learned at the synagogue, ate Mediterranean food, needed his feet to be washed, prayed, slept, bathed, and all the human experiences we know all too well. Knowing that Jesus was also fully human can sometimes make us uncomfortable....But that very discomfort is why John tells us Jesus is bread—earthly, cultivated, kneaded, human bread (pp. 33–34).

- Does knowing Jesus's parents, and other particulars of his earthly life, make him seem less divine? Why, or why not?
- Think about how bread differs from one culture to the next. How many different examples can you think of?
- Does the great variety of bread across the world contribute to the meaning of bread as a symbol for Jesus?
- Bread is shaped, worked, kneaded, baked. How does this formation by humans enrich our understanding of Jesus, when we consider that Jesus is "the bread of life"?

THE ACT: OVER AND OVER AGAIN

Divide your group into four teams and assign to each team one of the following Scriptures:

- John 5:1-18
- John 6:1-42
- John 9:1-41
- John 11:17-53

Say: Matt Rawle notes a pattern in these miracle stories: (1) interaction with the disciples, followed by (2) confusing questions, then (3) a miracle. Those receiving the miracle (4) experience initial confusion but ultimately (5) grow in their understanding of Jesus, while (6) others grow more skeptical. You may wish to list these in shorthand on a markerboard or large sheet of paper for easy reference.

Invite the teams to work together and identify the various parts of the pattern in their assigned passage. Allow them to work for 5–10 minutes, then call the whole group back together. Give each group an opportunity to report on what they found:

- Were they able to find all the parts of the pattern in their assigned passage?
- What variations did they find, if any (*changed order, more time spent on one part than others, and so on*)?

Read the following quote aloud:

These patterns exist in John's Gospel so that we might understand the interconnectedness of the Gospel as a whole, and the multiple dimensions of God's Incarnation in the person of Jesus (p. 38).

- What connections do you see between Jesus as the light of the world and the bread of life?
- How do both images, bread and light, contribute to a fuller understanding of who Jesus is?
- Do you see this pattern, or any others, as you reflect on your experience of faith? What might these patterns say about the larger story of what God is doing in your life?

THE PLAY: MANNA IN THE WILDERNESS

Invite a volunteer to read John 6:48-51.

- Why does Jesus seem to emphasize the difference between himself as the bread of life and the manna the Israelites ate?
- What does Jesus offer to the people that the manna did not provide for the Israelites?

Invite a second volunteer to read Exodus 16:1-21.

When we think of the manna in the wilderness, we often regard it as a positive miracle. Matt Rawle suggests that there may be more negative connotations in this miracle than are apparent at first glance (see pp. 39–42).

- How does it change your perspective to consider the manna as a tongue-in-cheek response from God to the Israelites' complaining?
- What parallels do you see between the crowd's response to Jesus and the Israelites' behavior in the wilderness?

CLOSING THE SESSION: YOUR ROLE

Read the following quote aloud:

In many ways "I am bread" feels like an opposite or complementary portrait with "I am light," but there is an intriguing overlap in the way we understand both. It's true that bread doesn't last forever and must be consumed before it spoils, and yet bread holds a timeless significance in the context of our worship. When we gather around the Lord's Table for Holy Communion, when we bring our gift of bread to the Table, God transforms our gift into an offering through which Christ's mysterious presence is made known. The bread reminds us that our gifts and talents, when offered in the context of God's work, take on a holy and timeless significance....Our role is to be nourished by Christ and to nourish one another through sacrificial giving, becoming a holy and living sacrifice for God. (p. 43)

- Jesus saying "I am the bread of life" calls to mind the sacrament of Holy Communion. How does our worship reflect both the human and the divine character of Jesus?
- What is the role of imperfection in our Christian worship? How do variation, struggle, and even imperfection in your life bear witness to Jesus?
- What hope or encouragement do you take from today's lesson and book chapter? What do you feel led to do in response?

CLOSING PRAYER

End with the following prayer or one of your own:

Lord Jesus, bread of life. We come to you today, human and imperfect, reflecting your humanity even as we seek from you the living bread that will nourish us forever. Grant us wisdom and boldness to bring ourselves to you, offering you what we have in the trust that you will take it and bless it with a timeless and holy significance. Amen.

I AM THE
GOOD SHEPHERD

PLANNING THE SESSION

SESSION GOALS

Through this session's discussion and activities, participants will
be encouraged to:

- understand how Jesus's identity as the Good Shepherd
  complements and deepens the picture we have of Jesus as
  light and bread;
- recognize the calling we have from Jesus to follow the
  Good Shepherd and feed our fellow sheep; and
- appreciate the symbolic resonances of the imagery of
  shepherd across the rest of John's Gospel and Scripture.

BIBLICAL FOUNDATION

- Psalm 23:1-6
- John 10:1-30
- John 21:1-19

PREPARATION

- Read chapter 3, "I Am the Good Sheperd," in *Jesus Revealed*, by Matt Rawle, making note of anything that stands out to you.
- Read through this Leader Guide session to familiarize yourself with it and to decide which questions you will cover.
- Read and reflect on the Biblical Foundation passages listed above.
- Preview the session 3 video and make arrangements to play it, using a DVD player or computer, during your session.
- Set up a markerboard or large sheet of paper for recording group members' ideas.
- Have a Bible, paper for taking notes, and a pen or pencil available for every participant.

OPENING THE SESSION

Greet and welcome participants as they arrive. Invite them to make a nametag and pick up either a Bible or a copy of *Jesus Revealed*, or both, if they did not bring their own.

Give any new members an opportunity to introduce themselves. Begin your discussion by playing a game of "This or That."

Ask everyone to stand up and move to an open area of the room, where they can move around a bit.

Explain the rules of the game: You will read several pairs of items, and people must indicate which one they are most like. For instance, are you more like a *pencil* or an *eraser*? There are no right answers, and people may decide based on whatever criteria makes sense to them. Have people move to the right side of the room if they are more like the first item, and to the left side of the room if they are more like the second item. (As an alternative, if you prefer not to stand up and move, you may have the group raise their right hand for the first item and their left hand for the second item.)

Read each pair of items below, giving everyone time to respond based on which item they are most like. After each pair, pick one person from each group to share why she or he is more like that item. Try to pick a different person each time if possible.

Are you more like a...

- sheep or goat
- glass of water or Magic Marker
- boat or plane
- tennis racket or baseball
- song or book

After several rounds, explain that you're going to play two more times. But this time, instead of answering for yourself, you're going to answer for Jesus. People must choose; they're not allowed to say both! Is Jesus more like a...

- shepherd or light
- shepherd or bread

Invite some discussion of what people chose, and why.

Remind the group that you have explored two I Am statements so far: "I am the light of the world" and "I am the bread of life." This week you'll look at a third statement: "I am the good shepherd."

OPENING PRAYER

Open with the following prayer or one of your own:

Lord God, open our eyes, ears, and hearts to you that we may see you as our Good Shepherd. Help us to hear and recognize your voice and respond to you in faithfulness. Call us by your name and lead us in your way; in Jesus's name we pray. Amen.

WATCH THE VIDEO

Play the video for session 3 using your DVD player or stream with Amplify Media. Discuss the following questions:

- What stood out to you as you watched the video? What words do you feel like you need to qualify with the word *good*?
- Say the opening of Psalm 23: "The LORD is my shepherd." What word do you emphasize? How does emphasizing different words enrich the meaning of this sentence?
- Jesus said, "My sheep hear my voice" (John 10:27). What are you hearing?
- What thoughts, feelings, or images came to you as you watched the ending clip, of artist Sarah Duet painting a picture inspired by "I am the good shepherd"?

Invite the group to keep both the video and the book in mind throughout the discussion below.

SCRIPTURE AND BOOK STUDY

THE SCENE: I AM THE GOOD SHEPHERD

Begin by asking the following questions:

- What does a shepherd do? What responsibilities does a shepherd have? What images or ideas come to mind when you think of a shepherd?
- How is Jesus like a shepherd? What layers does the symbol of shepherd add to our multilayered picture of Jesus?

Invite a volunteer to read John 10:1-6 and another to read John 10:7-16. Discuss:

- What characters does Jesus mention in these two sections?

Record the names of the characters on a markerboard or large sheet of paper as the group lists them. (Characters include thief, outlaw, shepherd, guard, sheep, stranger, hired hand, wolf.)

- How does the shepherd compare with the other characters listed?

Note that we actually have another I Am statement in the same passage: "I am the gate of the sheep" (10:7).

- How does the statement "I am the gate" relate to the one Jesus says a few verses later, "I am the good shepherd"?
- Taking these two images together, what seems to be central in what Jesus is communicating here?
- Is Jesus more like a gate or a shepherd? How does emphasizing one or the other change our perspective on who he is?

Invite the group to turn to the discussion on page 52, where Matt Rawle says that "Jesus's identity as a shepherd invokes at least three layers of symbolism."

- What are the three layers? (*pastoral identity, a ruler like David or Moses, and the divine*)
- Which one of them seems to be most in view here? Why?

Invite someone to read John 10:22-30. Discuss:

- Why do the people ask for Jesus to "tell us plainly" whether he is the Messiah?
- What sort of answer are the people hoping for?

- What does Jesus's response to them say about how his understanding of Messiah differs from theirs?

Conclude this section by reading the following quote aloud:

Much like a multiplane camera moves through a scene transforming a two-dimensional picture into an immersive, cohesive three-dimensional offering, "I am the good shepherd" combines "I am light" (divine, out there) and "I am bread" (ground up, human) into a single statement of identity. With this third statement, the two-dimensional contrast between divinity and humanity becomes a three-dimensional reality with Jesus's revelation that "I am the good shepherd." Jesus is fully human and fully divine, and he embodies the divine nature in the human world in this particular way: as a good shepherd who leads, guides, cares for, and provides for his sheep. (p. 53)

THE ACT: FEED MY SHEEP

Invite a volunteer to read John 21:9-19 aloud. Discuss:

- What does the detail of a "charcoal fire" in verse 9 (NRSV) signal?
- Matt Rawle notes that there is a loss when we turn away from Jesus. What details in the text point to this loss on Peter's part? What has been lost?
- How does Jesus's instruction to Peter, "feed my sheep" (verse 17), offer him redemption and hope?
- What does Jesus's command to Peter imply about our own calling and command from Jesus in the world?

THE PLAY: THE LORD IS MY SHEPHERD

Read Psalm 23 slowly aloud, inviting the group to close their eyes and pay close attention as you read. When you finish, invite the group to open their eyes and discuss the following questions:

- What imagery does the psalmist use?
- Which part or parts of Psalm 23 do you find most compelling? Why?
- How does that part enhance your view of Jesus as the "good shepherd"?
- What do you hear the psalm calling you to do, as one of the flock who follows the Good Shepherd?

CLOSING THE SESSION: YOUR ROLE

Recall the first I Am statement in John 10, "I am the gate" (verse 7). Jesus is the one by whom we commune with God—not in an exclusive way, but in a way that focuses our energy and attention on the one thing that matters.

Matt Rawle says that our role is "to plant ourselves at the gate of hope so we might hear the Good Shepherd's voice and call" (p. 67).

- What can you do to open your ears to the shepherd's voice?
- How can you position yourself in such a way that you lead others to the gate?

CLOSING PRAYER

Conclude your session by praying Psalm 23 together, using the text on pages 63–64 of *Jesus Revealed*.

I AM THE VINE

PLANNING THE SESSION

SESSION GOALS

Through this session's discussion and activities, participants will be encouraged to:

- recognize this I Am statement as one that incorporates us followers of Jesus into his identity;
- commit ourselves to cultivating our relationship with Jesus and with our fellow followers of Christ; and
- appreciate that connection to Jesus as the vine is the true way to live, even as Jesus himself will be crucified.

BIBLICAL FOUNDATION

- John 15:1-17
- Philippians 1:18-26

PREPARATION

- Read chapter 4, "I Am the Vine" in *Jesus Revealed*, by Matt Rawle, making note of anything that stands out to you.
- Read through this Leader Guide session to familiarize yourself with it and to decide which questions you will cover.
- Read and reflect on the Biblical Foundation passages listed above.
- Preview the session 4 video and make arrangements to play it, using a DVD player or computer, during your session.
- Set up a markerboard or large sheet of paper for recording group members' ideas.
- Have a Bible, paper for taking notes, and a pen or pencil available for every participant.

OPENING THE SESSION

Greet and welcome participants as they arrive. Invite them to make a nametag and pick up either a Bible or a copy of *Jesus Revealed*, or both, if they did not bring their own.

Give any new members an opportunity to introduce themselves. *Briefly* recap last week's lesson and mention that today's session is on the I Am statement "I am the vine; you are the branches." Ask the following questions to begin your discussion:

- Name a trait that you have inherited. Who did you inherit it from? How do you feel about it?
- How has your life up to now brought that trait out or diminished it? Is it something you seek to cultivate or suppress? Why?

Say: Early in today's chapter, Matt Rawle shares a surprising discovery about his ancestry. He has an equal amount of Norwegian DNA and Filipino DNA, despite a long-standing affinity for

Norwegian culture. He writes, "We cannot choose our inheritance, but we can choose which inheritances we cultivate and which we will strive to overcome" (p. 73).

We have inherited a relationship with Jesus, and a relationship with one another through Jesus. It's up to us to cultivate and nurture that relationship. That's part of what Jesus tells us when he says, "I am the vine; you are the branches" (John 15:5).

OPENING PRAYER

Open with the following prayer, or one of your own.

Lord Jesus, you are the vine. We are the branches. Strengthen our connection with you, that we may draw spiritual nourishment from you. Show us our connection with the community of faith and give us grace and love for one another; in your name we pray. Amen.

WATCH THE VIDEO

Play the video for session 4 using your DVD player or stream with Amplify Media. Discuss the following questions:

- What stood out to you as you watched the video?
- Matt Rawle says that we can't choose what we inherit, but we can choose what parts of our inheritance we will cultivate. What parts of your faith tradition have you inherited? How do you choose to cultivate them?
- What do we give up when we are connected to Christ, the true vine? What do we gain?
- What thoughts, feelings, or images came to you as you watched the ending clip, of artist Sarah Duet painting a picture inspired by "I am the vine"?

Invite the group to keep both the video and the book in mind throughout the discussion below.

SCRIPTURE AND BOOK STUDY

THE SCENE: I AM THE VINE

Invite a volunteer to read John 15:1-8. Explain that this passage is part of a section of John known as Jesus's "farewell discourse," which runs from John 14 to John 17. This section contains a series of speeches from Jesus to the disciples after the Last Supper. Ask the following questions:

- How would you describe the relationship between the vine (Jesus), the vineyard keeper (the Father), and the branches (the disciples, us) in these verses?
- What does it mean to "produce fruit"? What is our role in producing fruit, based on Jesus's teaching here?
- How do you respond to the idea of being pruned or trimmed?

Say: Rawle notes that pruning or trimming can be equated with cleansing and suggests not punishment but refining or correction. He writes,

> It's not that some people bear fruit and others don't; rather, it's that we contain within ourselves that which bears fruit and that which doesn't....It is the power of the Holy Spirit working within all of us to prune away what is harmful for good fruit production. (p. 75)

- What in your life might the keeper of the vineyard need to prune? What about within your community of faith?
- How can you cooperate with the vineyard keeper to cultivate those parts of you (or of the faith community) that bear fruit?

Invite someone to read John 15:9-17. Discuss:

- Jesus says, "You didn't choose me, but I chose you" (verse 16). If we don't choose to be attached to the vine, what role do we play? How are we to respond?

- Not choosing the vine also means we don't choose our fellow branches. How does our union with Christ, the vine, affect our relationship with our fellow Christians?
- How does our relationship with other "branches" affect our ability to bear fruit?

Call attention to pages 76–79, beginning with, "For a time, most of my friends were obsessed with the PBS program *Downton Abbey*." Use Rawle's reflections here to guide your discussion of the following questions:

- Jesus's image of vine and branches might suggest a hierarchy, with the vine on top and the branches below. What parts of John 15:9-17 contrast with a hierarchical view?
- How does it change things to view the vine and the vineyard keeper as a source of life rather than as a seat of power or judgment?
- Do we sustain the vine even as the vine sustains us, or is it more of a one-way relationship? Why?

THE ACT: COMMUNITY

Read aloud the following quotation:

God as vineyard keeper cultivates and prunes the vine. This pruning is a means of cleansing the vine itself, but the cleansing isn't so that the vine will perpetually live. Quite the opposite. The vine itself will be cut down. (p. 80)

- Jesus is the vine; we are the branches. What does it mean for us, then, that the vine is cut down—that Jesus was crucified?
- What does the Crucifixion say about the life Jesus offers to us? What do we lose by being connected to the vine? What do we gain?

Invite a volunteer to read Philippians 1:18-26. Discuss:

- How would you describe Paul's "thinking-out-loud" struggle in these verses?
- What is the gain that Paul sees in death?
- If living means to serve Christ, what kind of life does Paul expect? What does that mean for the way we should expect to live?
- How does our service to Christ bring us in community with others?

THE PLAY: THE WINE OUTPOURED

Read aloud the following quotation, then discuss:

At some point, no matter how vibrant the vine, the grapes need to be harvested for wine. The grapes will be gathered, crushed underfoot, and bottled for fermentation. But then the wine will be shared around a table as a centerpiece of hospitality and welcome. I wonder if, when Jesus said, "I am the vine; you are the branches," and "No one has greater love than to give up one's life for one's friends" (John 15:5, 13), he had wine in mind.... When we meditate on how we gather around the Lord's Table for Holy Communion, we begin to see the beauty of our connectedness as vine and branches. (p. 83)

- How does the wine of Communion point to our connection to one another as the body of Christ?
- In this section, Matt Rawle points to both the prophetic and the priestly aspects of our connection to one another. What is the difference between the two? Which one, if either, seems to be more of an emphasis in your faith community?
- How do we balance truth and necessary confrontation with joy and comfort in our life together? How is Christ a source of both?

- Rawle suggests that peace is the central feature of our union with Christ as the vine. When have you seen examples of peace that are either too stringent or too shallow?
- How do we maintain a community in which true peace prevails?

CLOSING THE SESSION: YOUR ROLE

Call attention to the closing section of this chapter, "Your Role: When Gift Becomes Offering." Discuss:

- What is the difference between a gift and an offering?
- In what ways are we called to give ourselves as offerings to one another?
- What does Christ do with our offerings of ourselves? How does that represent the way to life?

Think back to the multilayered picture of Jesus we get through the I Am statements: Light representing the divine, bread representing the human, good shepherd bringing both together. Now, the image of vine and branches incorporates us into the picture.

- What does it say about God, and God's relationship with humanity, that we have a role to play in revealing Christ?

CLOSING PRAYER

Close with the following prayer, or one of your own:

Lord Jesus, thank you for choosing us. Thank you for joining us to yourself and sustaining us with your very life. Thank you also for the gift of one another, and for the opportunity to produce fruit for your kingdom alongside the community of faith. Nourish and strengthen us, Lord, so that we might offer ourselves to you, to one another, and to the world; in your name we pray. Amen.

I AM THE WAY, THE TRUTH, AND THE LIFE

PLANNING THE SESSION

SESSION GOALS

Through this session's discussion and activities, participants will be encouraged to:

- understand the multiple layers in the metaphor of Jesus as the way, or the road;
- recognize the difficult and costly way that Jesus sets before us; and
- explore the relationship between the way of suffering and the way that leads to life.

BIBLICAL FOUNDATION

- John 14:1-14
- John 20:24-29
- 1 John 4:12-16

PREPARATION

- Read chapter 5, "I Am the Way, the Truth, and the Life," in *Jesus Revealed*, by Matt Rawle, making note of anything that stands out to you.
- Read through this Leader Guide session to familiarize yourself with it and to decide which questions you will cover.
- Read and reflect on the Biblical Foundation passages listed above.
- Preview the session 5 video and make arrangements to play it, using a DVD player or computer, during your session.
- Set up a markerboard or large sheet of paper for recording group members' ideas.
- Have a Bible, paper for taking notes, and a pen or pencil available for every participant.

OPENING THE SESSION

Greet and welcome participants as they arrive. Invite them to make a nametag and pick up either a Bible or a copy of *Jesus Revealed*, or both, if they did not bring their own.

Briefly recap last week's lesson and mention that today's session is on the I Am statement "I am the way, the truth, and the life." **Ask the following questions to begin your discussion:**

- When was the last time you took a road trip? How far away did you go? How long did the trip take you? Who went the farthest? (*Note that we're talking about a road trip, traveling by car rather than by plane or some other means.*)

- Was the trip enjoyable, or difficult, or both? What made it so?
- How did you decide what route to take?
- How would it have affected your trip if there had been only one possible route, no matter how long or difficult or heavily trafficked?

Say: Today we are going to discuss Jesus's fifth I Am statement, "I am the way, the truth, and the life." As we will discover, the way that Jesus indicates is a hard path that leads toward the cross. As much as we wish there were another way, there isn't. Yet it is the way of the cross that is also the way of life.

OPENING PRAYER

Begin with the following prayer or one of your own:

Lord Jesus, we believe in God and in you. We trust that you are the way, and the truth, and the life. Give us courage to travel this way, following you, with untroubled hearts, however hard the road may become. Help us see you in our fellow travelers. And teach us to love, which is the way both of suffering and of life; in your name we pray. Amen.

WATCH THE VIDEO

Play the video for session 5 using your DVD player or stream with Amplify Media. Discuss the following questions:

- What stood out to you as you watched the video?
- "I am the way…" Why do we tend to read this "I am" statement more literally than the others?

- Matt Rawle reminds us that the way of Jesus is the way of the cross. How does this change your understanding of Jesus's statement "I am the way, the truth, and the life"?
- What thoughts, feelings, or images came to you as you watched the ending clip, of artist Sarah Duet painting a picture inspired by "I am the way"?

Invite the group to keep both the video and the book in mind throughout the discussion below.

SCRIPTURE AND BOOK STUDY

THE SCENE: I AM THE WAY

- What are some well-known last words you're familiar with?
- Have you ever given thought to what you'd like your last words to be? If so, what would you like to say?

Invite a volunteer to read John 14:1-7.

Say: Jesus's statement "I am the way, the truth, and the life" comes near the beginning of his "farewell discourse," a lengthy section of teaching that we also discussed last week. These are some of the last words of Jesus, the things he wanted to be sure to communicate to his disciples before his arrest and crucifixion.

Maybe that's why we regard Jesus's statement here with a bit more significance than the others. It comes near the beginning of his farewell discourse. Discuss:

- What does Matt Rawle mean when he says on page 96 that "I am the way, the truth, and the life" has been interpreted to mean "an exclusionary model of salvation defined once and for all by Jesus himself"?
- Based on Rawle's discussion and what we've learned so far in this study, should we interpret "the way" literally

or metaphorically? If it's a metaphor, what does that
metaphor point to?

- Do you think Jesus had in mind an exclusive way?
  Why or why not?
- Why might we want there to be another way to God
  for ourselves?

THE ACT: THOMAS, THE ONE WHO CAME BACK

Invite a volunteer to read John 14:8-14.

Say: Matt Rawle points to the real image of a Roman road, which
Jesus's words "I am the way" would have evoked. Roads represented
Rome's ingenuity, but also its dominance—the roads were often sites
where criminals and dissidents were crucified.

Read the following quotation aloud:

Jesus isn't talking about a meditative pathway or a set of ideals
in order to find God; rather Jesus is talking about a way that the
oppressed Jewish community knew all too well. A road to walk, a
road on which suffering was possible and even likely. (p. 97)

- When confronted with this "way," why does Philip
  respond the way that he does (verse 8)?
- What does Philip hope to gain by seeing the Father?
- What sort of alternative "way" is Philip hoping for?
- Where do you see this tendency in your own spiritual
  life? In your congregation or in our world today?
- How would Jesus respond to us, based on his response
  to Philip?

Invite a volunteer to read John 20:24-29. Call attention to pages
99–100, beginning with "Could it be that Thomas wasn't there with
the other disciples specifically because he wasn't afraid?" Discuss:

- Have you ever considered that Thomas's absence when
  Jesus appeared to the other disciples was a sign not of
  doubt or discouragement, but of courage?

- How do you respond to the possibility that Thomas doubts not whether Jesus has been raised, but whether the way of suffering is really the way he should follow?
- How does Jesus's resurrection, scars and all, confirm that the way of the cross really is the way of life?
- What response does this call for from us?
- What is the difference between asking to see the Father and walking the path of suffering that Jesus himself walked?

THE PLAY: SEEING GOD

Invite a volunteer to read 1 John 4:12-16 aloud. Discuss:

- If Scripture is full of accounts of those who see God—including Abraham and Moses—what does the author of 1 John mean by saying that no one has seen God?
- How does love reveal God to us?
- Conversely, how does the absence of love prevent us from seeing God clearly?
- Jesus tells Philip that "whoever has seen me has seen the Father" (John 14:9). How does Jesus reveal God to us? What is the role of love in this revelation?
- Understanding the I Am statements has been an exercise in seeing Jesus more clearly. In what ways have the I Am statements drawn us ever deeper into the life of love?
- Is it possible to love fully in the way of Jesus without the witness of Scripture? Why or why not?

CLOSING THE SESSION: YOUR ROLE

Matt Rawle points to the suffering inherent in love.

- What does he mean by this?

- How do you see love prompting us to a way of self-sacrifice and even pain?
- Do you agree that God's creation of the world was an act of suffering? Why or why not? What is the nature of this suffering?
- To what extent does the suffering we experience in life—in all its forms—stem from love?
- Matt Rawle argues that the way of suffering and the way of love are ultimately one and the same. Do you agree with this? Why or why not?
- What do you feel God calling you to do in order to follow the way, the truth, and the life more closely?

CLOSING PRAYER

Close your session with the following prayer, or one of your own.

Lord Jesus, we confess that we often want an easier way—a way that doesn't challenge us, that doesn't ask much of us, that comforts us without requiring our commitment. So often we want to see the Father without following you and without loving our neighbors. Forgive us. Grant us the strength and clarity of vision we need and grant us the love we need to follow you in the way that leads to truth and life, the way of the cross, the way of love. Amen.

6

I AM THE RESURRECTION AND THE LIFE

PLANNING THE SESSION

SESSION GOALS

Through this session's discussion and activities, participants will be encouraged to:

- recognize that all the I Am statements point toward the resurrection of Jesus;
- explore how the Resurrection makes us unlearn everything we know about the world; and
- understand our role in God's story, who we are and how we are called to live because Jesus was raised.

BIBLICAL FOUNDATION

- John 11:17-46
- John 20:1-18
- 1 Samuel 28:3-25

PREPARATION

- Read chapter 6, "I Am the Resurrection and the Life," in *Jesus Revealed*, by Matt Rawle, making note of anything that stands out to you.
- Read through this Leader Guide session to familiarize yourself with it and to decide which questions you will cover.
- Read and reflect on the Biblical Foundation passages listed above.
- Preview the session 6 video and make arrangements to play it, using a DVD player or computer, during your session.
- Set up a markerboard or large sheet of paper for recording group members' ideas.
- Have a Bible, paper for taking notes, and a pen or pencil available for every participant.

OPENING THE SESSION

Greet and welcome participants as they arrive. Invite them to make a nametag and pick up either a Bible or a copy of *Jesus Revealed*, or both, if they did not bring their own.

Briefly recap last week's lesson and review the previous I Am statements you've studied so far:

- I am the light of the world.
- I am the bread of life.
- I am the good shepherd.

- I am the gate of the sheep.
- I am the vine; you are the branches.
- I am the way, the truth, and the life.

Say: Together, these I Am statements paint a rich, multilayered picture of who Jesus is. Discuss:

- Which of the I Am statements taught you something new about who Jesus is? What did it teach you?
- Which of the I Am statements resonates with you the most? Why?

Mention that today's session is on the I Am statement "I am the resurrection and the life," and that all the previous I Am statements find their culmination in this one. The Resurrection changes everything.

OPENING PRAYER

Pray the following prayer or one of your own:

Lord God, over these last several weeks you have revealed to us so much about who you are. Thank you for the teachings of Jesus, his miracles, and the words of Scripture that preserve and communicate them to us today. Guide us now as we explore the mystery and great hope of the Resurrection. Help us to trust that Jesus is the resurrection and the life; in Jesus's name we pray. Amen.

WATCH THE VIDEO

Play the video for session 6 using your DVD player or stream with Amplify Media. Discuss the following questions:

- What stood out to you as you watched the video?
- The resurrection of Jesus changes things. What does the resurrection of Jesus force you to unlearn?

- We are a part of the Resurrection story. What can you do to participate in this story, living as if your life matters?
- What thoughts, feelings, or images came to you as you watched the ending clip, of artist Sarah Duet painting a picture inspired by "I am the resurrection and the life"?

Invite the group to keep both the video and the book in mind throughout the discussion below.

SCRIPTURE AND BOOK STUDY

THE SCENE: I AM THE RESURRECTION

- Have you ever had to unlearn something—perhaps something you remembered incorrectly, or a bad habit you had to break? What was it? How did you go about it?

Read the following quotation aloud:

The raising of Lazarus in John 11, in which Jesus proclaims, "I am the resurrection," is an exercise in checking our assumptions, unlearning what we think we know, and "unbinding" our understanding for how God is at work in the world. (p. 117)

Say: One of the assumptions we make about life is that death is final. Life is finite and will one day end.

- Is death something that you think about every day? Every week? How often do you think about it?
- Think about your daily habits, or your weekly, monthly, or yearly patterns. What assumptions about death and life are built into those habits?
- How would it change things if you committed to living as if death truly wasn't the end?

Invite a volunteer to read John 11:17-27. Discuss:

- How would you describe the interaction between Martha and Jesus? What feelings and attitudes seem to characterize the scene?
- Do you think Martha believes that Jesus is the resurrection and the life? Why or why not?
- What do you think Martha and Mary want or expect Jesus to do?

Invite another volunteer to read John 11:38-46. Discuss:

- How did the raising of Lazarus change things for Mary and Martha? What about for the others who were watching? What about for the religious leaders?
- Matt Rawle says that "if death is not the end of our story, then there is nothing to fear, and our daily life should reflect this life-giving, reckless abandon" (p. 120). Do you agree with this idea? Why or why not?
- What can you do to live as if the Resurrection is true?
- Jesus commands for Lazarus's binds to be taken off. What binds you and keeps you from living a life of fearless trust in the Resurrection? What would it mean for you to live an unbound life?

THE ACT: SHE'S ONLY SLEEPING

Invite a volunteer to read Mark 5:21-43.

Say: When Jesus goes to heal Jairus's daughter, he is delayed because of the need to heal someone else.

- How do you think Jairus reacted to Jesus's decision to stop on the way to heal his daughter?
- How does the truth of the Resurrection change our relationship with time?

- What kinds of things cause you to be in a hurry? How do you feel in these situations? (*Note*: Encourage the group to think of serious examples as well as those that are more mundane. Traffic causes us to hurry, but so do life goals such as going back to school or seeking a promotion at work.)
- What would a different relationship with time offer you in these situations?
- How does the hope of resurrection set these other situations in perspective? How might you approach them differently if you were to take the Resurrection seriously?

THE PLAY: THE MEDIUM OF EN-DOR

Say: Jesus's raising of Lazarus wasn't the only time someone in Scripture was raised from the dead. In the Book of 1 Samuel, Saul had a medium raise the prophet Samuel from the dead so that Saul could talk with Samuel.

Invite a volunteer to read 1 Samuel 28:3-25. Call attention to the section "The Play: The Medium of En-dor" on pages 122–126 and Matt Rawle's interpretation of this story.

- What did Saul hope to gain by consulting Samuel? Was he successful? Why or why not?
- What fundamental differences are there between the medium's raising of Samuel and Jesus's raising of Lazarus? What similarities are there?
- Did things change for Saul as a result of his consultation of Samuel? What about for Lazarus, after Jesus raised him from the dead?
- How does the resurrection of Jesus go beyond both the raising of Samuel and the raising of Lazarus? What is the relationship of these two earlier stories to the Resurrection on Easter?

CLOSING THE SESSION: YOUR ROLE

Invite a volunteer to read John 20:1-18. Instruct the volunteer to read the words slowly, and have the other participants close their eyes and listen to the account of the Resurrection.

Remind the participants of the seven I Am statements (see the list, on pageS 57–58 of this Leader Guide). Invite the volunteer to read John 20:1-18 again, and this time have the participants listen for echoes of the I Am statements in the Resurrection account. For instance, Jesus speaking to Mary might echo "I am the good shepherd" because the sheep hear the shepherd's voice. When the Resurrection story has been read a second time, discuss:

- What echoes of the I Am statements did you hear?
  (If your group has trouble, consult the section "Your Role: I Am, Because This Is, Because You Are," on pages 126–131 for guidance.)
- What response does the resurrection of Jesus call forth from Mary?
- What response does the Resurrection call forth from us?
- How do the I Am statements we've learned about enrich your understanding of the resurrection of Jesus? How do they sharpen your perspective on the life we are called to lead as followers of Christ?
- What will you do differently as a result of this study?

CLOSING PRAYER

Thank your group members for joining you in this study and encourage them to keep growing in faith and live as if the Resurrection is true. Close your study with the following prayer, or one of your own:

Christ Jesus, you are the light of the world. You are the bread of life. You are the gate and the good shepherd. You are the vine and we are the branches. You are the way, the truth, and the life. You are the resurrection and the life. Because of who you are, we know who we are. We are your followers, whose path you illuminate. We are your followers, whom you sustain and guide. We are your followers, whom you connect to yourself and to one another. We are your followers on the way of suffering, which is the way of life. We are your followers forever, because death is not the end. Lord Jesus, we love you. We trust you. Amen.

CPSIA information can be obtained
at www.ICGtesting.com
Printed in the USA
LVHW040944120622
720931LV00006B/19